Meet Memo

I'm **Memo** the **Me**mory **Mo**nster.
I have an enormous brain.
It's made up of all your lovely memories.
It grows whenever you learn things.

I love brains that have fun learning things.
Is your brain like that?
If it is you'll help to keep me strong and healthy.
So do play all the games in this book and learn lots of new things with your magic memory.

MEET BRAMBLE

I'm Bramble, the Wizard's special cat.

Being a cat, I've always been very clever anyway.
Now that the Wizard's taught me all his Magic Memory secrets, I am brilliant!

The Wizard has asked me to show Charlie and Holly how to remember things.

They are sometimes very slow.
They spoil most of the memory games I play with them.

I bet you'll be much quicker than them.

WOOF!
I'm Charlie!
I'm a yellow Labrador and a very happy waggy tailed dog.
The best time of my day is eating my dinner.
It doesn't last long enough, though.
The next best time is breakfast.
That's over too quickly too.
When I'm not eating I love chasing a ball.
Bramble's decided to show me how to remember important things.
Will you help if I get stuck?
It might mean I can find more food!

WOOF!   I'm Holly!
I'm a brown Labrador and a very happy waggy tailed dog.
Charlie's my best friend.
I love my breakfasts and dinners – and any other food I can find.
Bramble plays lots of memory games with us.
She's very clever and always wins.
She's a bit unfair as well....**gold** fish **are** fish.
She said I was 'OUT' just because I said **fish** instead of **gold fish**.
But playing games fills in the time between meals and walks.
Guess what...we're now getting really good at learning things.

Outside the castle of the Grand Wizard of Spells, on a day just like today, all is not well....
GRAND WIZARD of SPELLS

GRAND WIZARD of SPELLS

Help!

Memo looks really poorly.
Yes, she does, doesn't she. Memo, what's wrong my dear?
Children don't want to learn things anymore. Their brains are not working properly. Their lazy Brian Cells just slob around all day. When their Brian Cells forget how to remember things......I WILL DIE.
Here are some lazy Brian Cells. They can't be bothered to learn anything. No wonder poor Memo is dying.
Bramble! We must save Memo. Got any ideas?
How about showing children how to use their Magic Memories?
That's a great idea. Mmmmm....Whenever they learn something new, they'll save a bit of Memo - and you, Bramble, can teach Charlie and Holly.

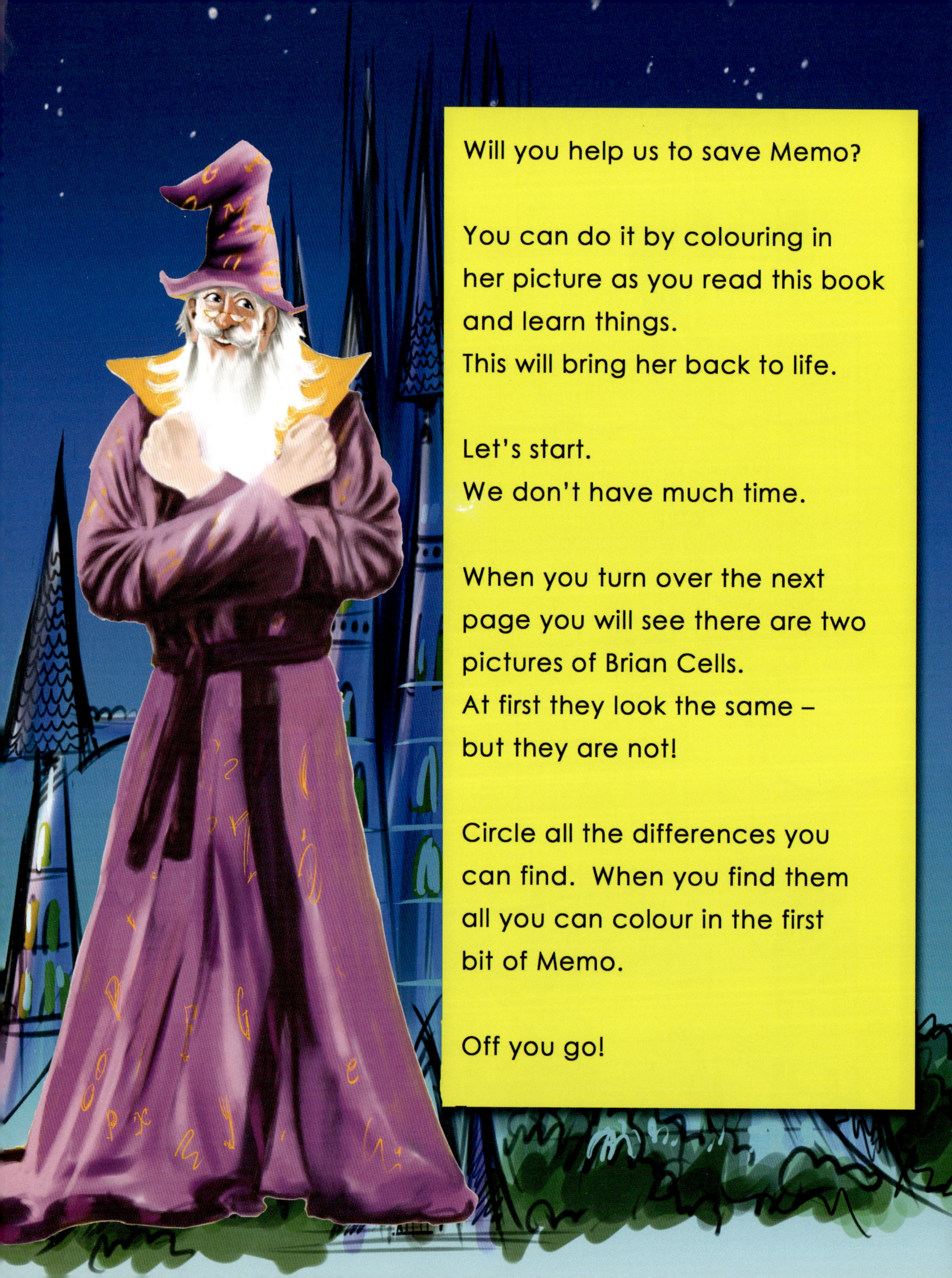

Will you help us to save Memo?

You can do it by colouring in
her picture as you read this book
and learn things.
This will bring her back to life.

Let's start.
We don't have much time.

When you turn over the next
page you will see there are two
pictures of Brian Cells.
At first they look the same –
but they are not!

Circle all the differences you
can find. When you find them
all you can colour in the first
bit of Memo.

Off you go!

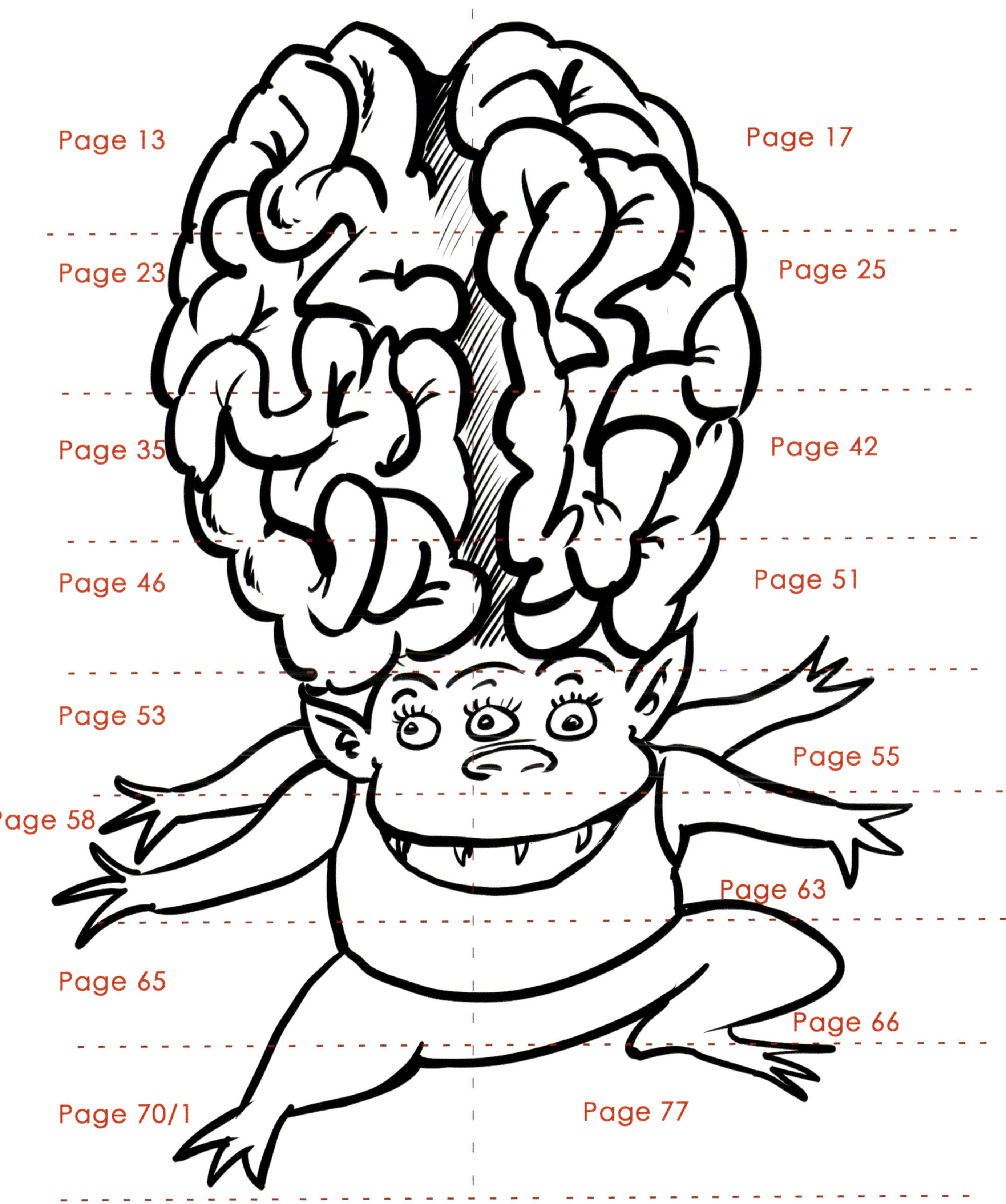

You can download a printable version of this page and other games from www.memorysue.com

Spot the difference

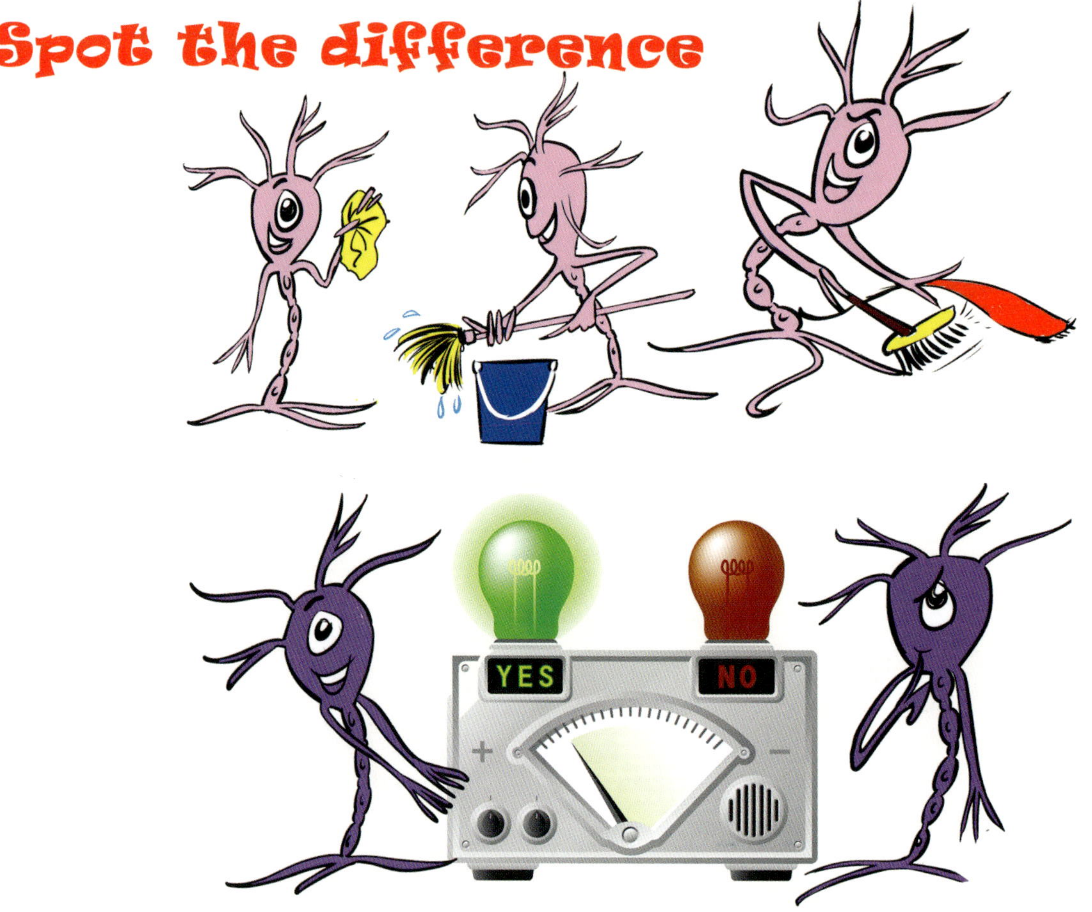

Look carefully at the pictures on these two pages.

Circle all the differences you can find.

Magic Memory Tip

Put your finger below the first Brian Cell in the first picture.
Then put your finger below the same Brian Cell in
the second picture.
Go backwards and forwards looking at every little
bit of him, taking photos in your mind:

- his hair (count the strands)

- his head, his middle

- his fingers (count them)

- his legs / toes (count them).

Do this for every Brian Cell in turn.
Then take photos of all the bits of the YES NO machine.

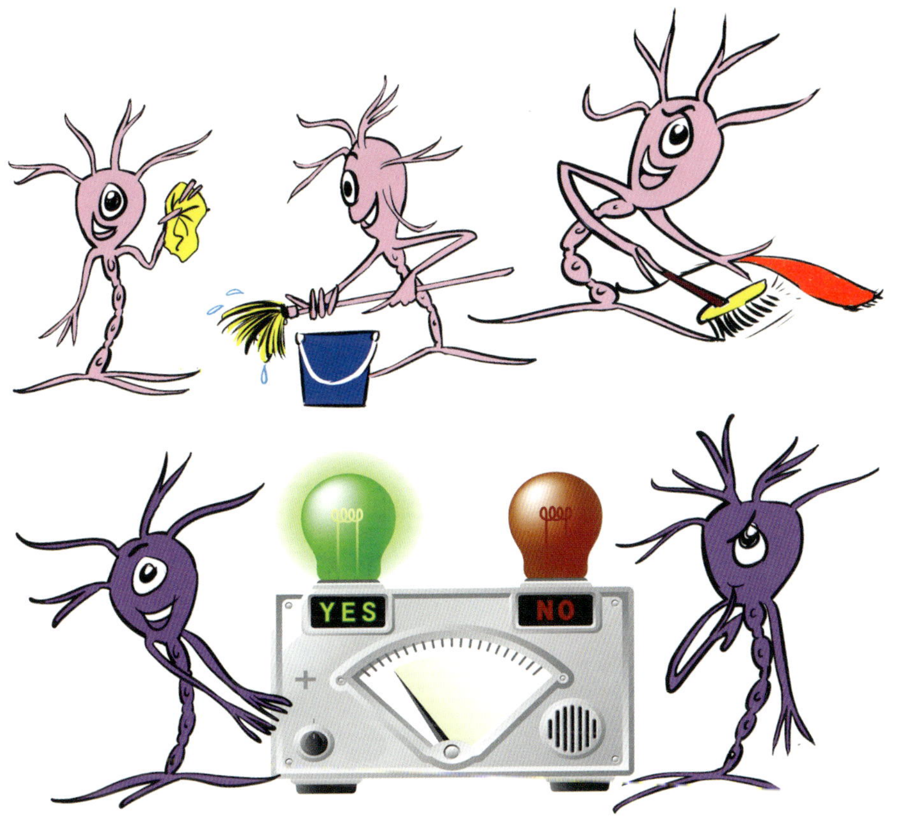

Did you find all ten differences? Excellent!

Check them with the answers at the back of the book.

Then colour in the first bit of Memo.

Why Brains need to forget things

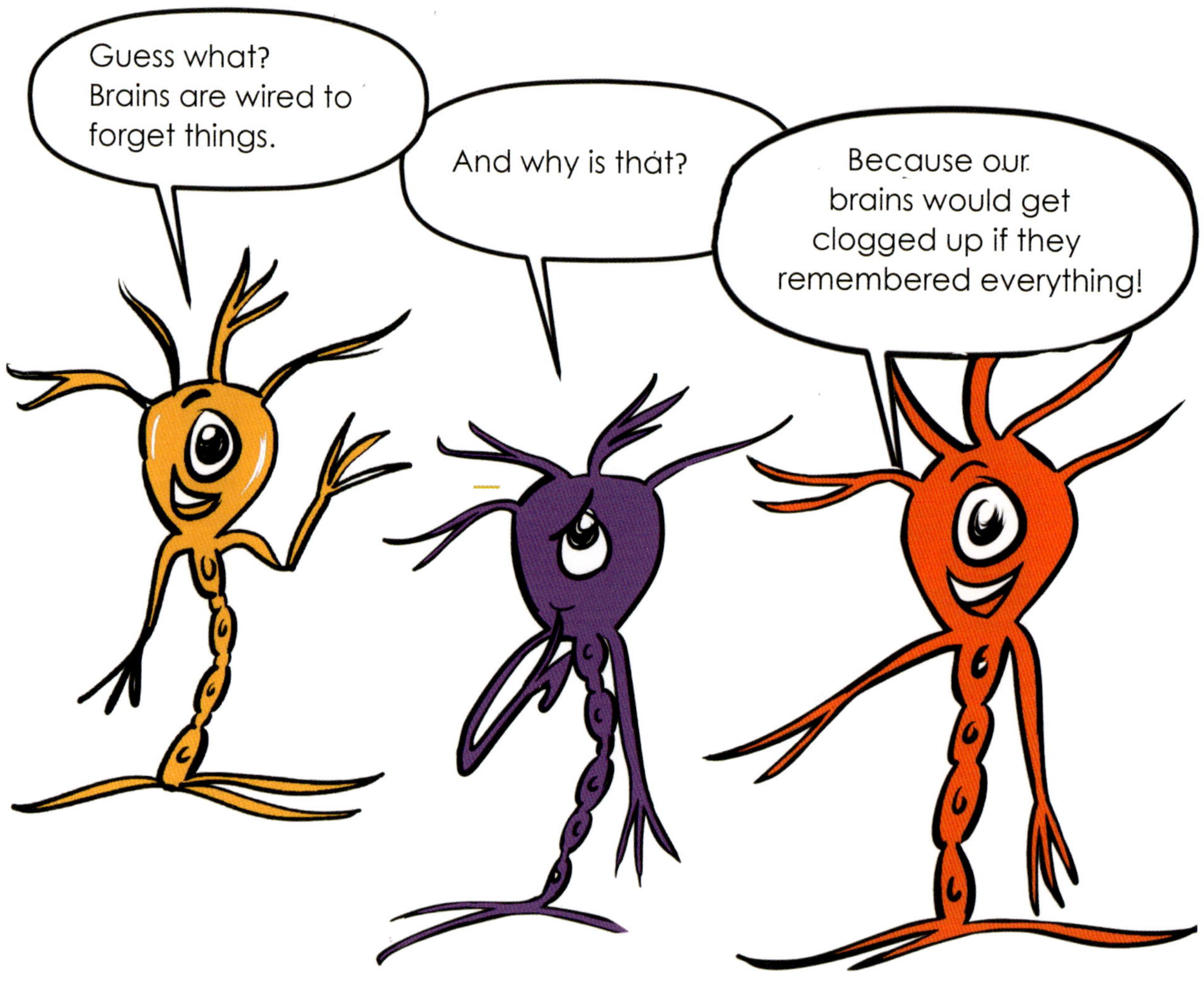

OVERLOAD!

Magic Brain Fact.

Brains are very clever.

They are a bit like computers.

Every night, when you're asleep,

all the rubbish is cleared away.

Things you want to keep are tidied away

so you can find them the next day...

While you are asleep your Brian Cells are
busy throwing away all the rubbish.

As you read this book, and play the games, you will learn
how to tell your Brian Cells what you want them to remember.

Quiz

When you are fast asleep at night your Brian Cells
are busy. Which of these things do they do
(write the letter **T** for True or **F** for False):

.... They put things you've learned in a safe place so you can find
them the next day.

.... They are also fast asleep and snoring.

.... They throw all the rubbish away.

.... They throw away things they think you don't want to
remember.

.... They have a party with the Food Brians and eat lots of
crisps.

.... They put spellings you've learned in a safe place
so you can find them the next day.

.... They go out and have a party.

.... They give your brain a really good clean.

.... They make sure that your brain is
sparkly clean with plenty of room
for all the new stuff you want to
learn the next day.

Check your answers with those at the back
of the book. Are they right? Great!
Colour in the next bit of Memo.

Charlie's Nightmare

Charlie has a nightmare. He remembers everything....and he doesn't want to. He can't find his latest and favourite bone.

What's up, Charlie?
I've had the most horrible dream.
Oh I'm sorry. Never mind. You're awake now and safe with me. What happened?
Overload! Overload!
Well I dreamed that I remembered EVERYTHING! I don't want to remember everything.....just the important things.
What did you want to remember?
Where I'd buried my newest and best ever bone in the whole world. I knew where all my old bones were. I knew when I buried them. I even remembered when I dug them up. But with all that stuff clogging up my brain, I couldn't remember where my newest bone was.
Don't worry Charlie. It was only a dream. In real life your brain forgets things you don't need. Then you can find important stuff easily.

You already have magic memories.
You remember birthdays and where you live don't you?
Yes!
BIRTHDAY GIRL
HAPPY BIRTHDAY HOLLY
CHARLIE
Yes!
So you remember loads of important stuff already without even trying?
Yes.

Bramble remembers important things in life

Charlie and Holly remember important things too....

CHOP! CHOP! CHOP!

Aha! Chopping noises means the chance of extra food! We'll just sneak in and sit nice and quietly.

Ooops!

We'll remember this, won't we, Holly!
Oh yes!

Quiz

To save a bit more of Memo, fill in the blanks and circle Yes or No to the questions below.

Do you remember the important things in your life?

Your name _______________________________

Your birthday _______________________________

Your friends' names _______________________________

____

____

Do you know where spoons are kept at home?   Yes/No

Where you live?   Yes/No

Do you know where to find your coat peg in school? Yes/No

Do you remember to take your pencil case to school
(most days, anyway)?   Yes/No

I bet that if you close your eyes you can name nearly everyone in your class.

How many names is that? _______   *Wow!*

Have you filled in the blanks and answered 'Yes' to everything else?

Fantastic! You already have a brilliant memory!

Colour in the next bit of Memo.

Find the Odd One Out

All these Brian Cells look the same.
But one is different. Which one is it?

Magic Memory Tip

Put a finger of your left hand below the first Brian Cell.

Take a photo of a little bit of him then look at the same bit of all the other Brian Cells in turn:

- fingers (count them)
- toes (count them)
- head
- middle
- hair (count the strands).

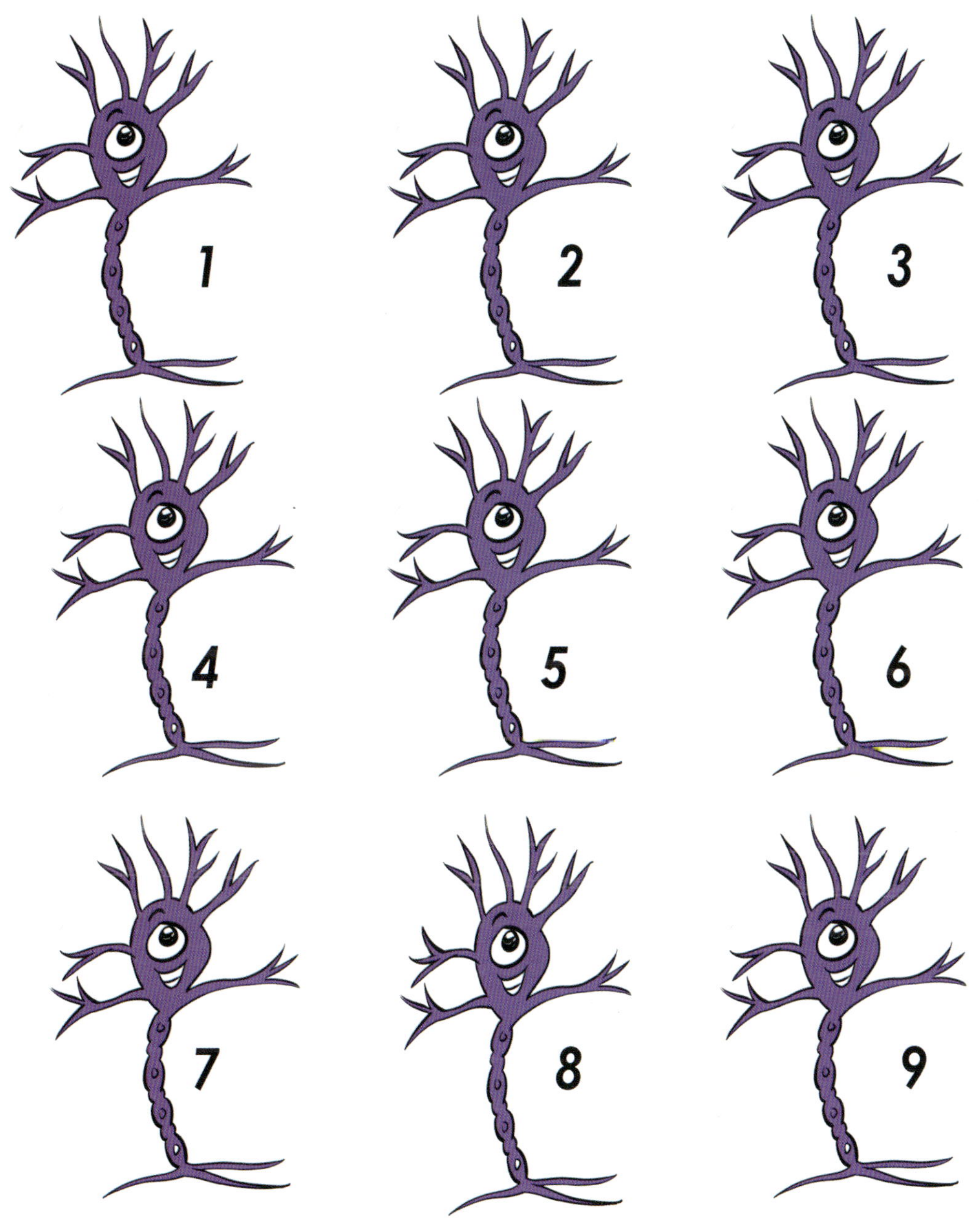

Did you find the one that's different?

Excellent! Colour in the next bit of Memo!

Bramble plays 'Spot the Difference'

Bramble's showing Charlie and Holly a new game

Bramble shows Holly how to play Find the Odd One Out.
Holly is still very slow and needs some help from you.

What has changed?

How to play:

- Everyone starts in one room.
- Choose one person to go out.
- Change ONE thing in the room while they're out.
- They then have two minutes to find it when they come back.
- If they're right, they choose the next person to go out.
- If they're wrong, the previous person chooses someone.

Things to move:

- Move a CD to the other side of the room.
- Turn a photograph frame round so you can't see the picture.
- Move a chair.
- Turn a book upside down.
- Pick up something small and put it into someone's pocket.

Magic Memory Tips to remember everything before you go out

- Starting in one corner look at everything in the room very carefully.
- Take lots of photos in your mind.
- Whisper things to yourself such as 'Three books on the table.'

Magic Memory Tips to find what's changed

- Start in the same corner to look at everything very carefully again.
- Work out what people are looking at. They often give it away!

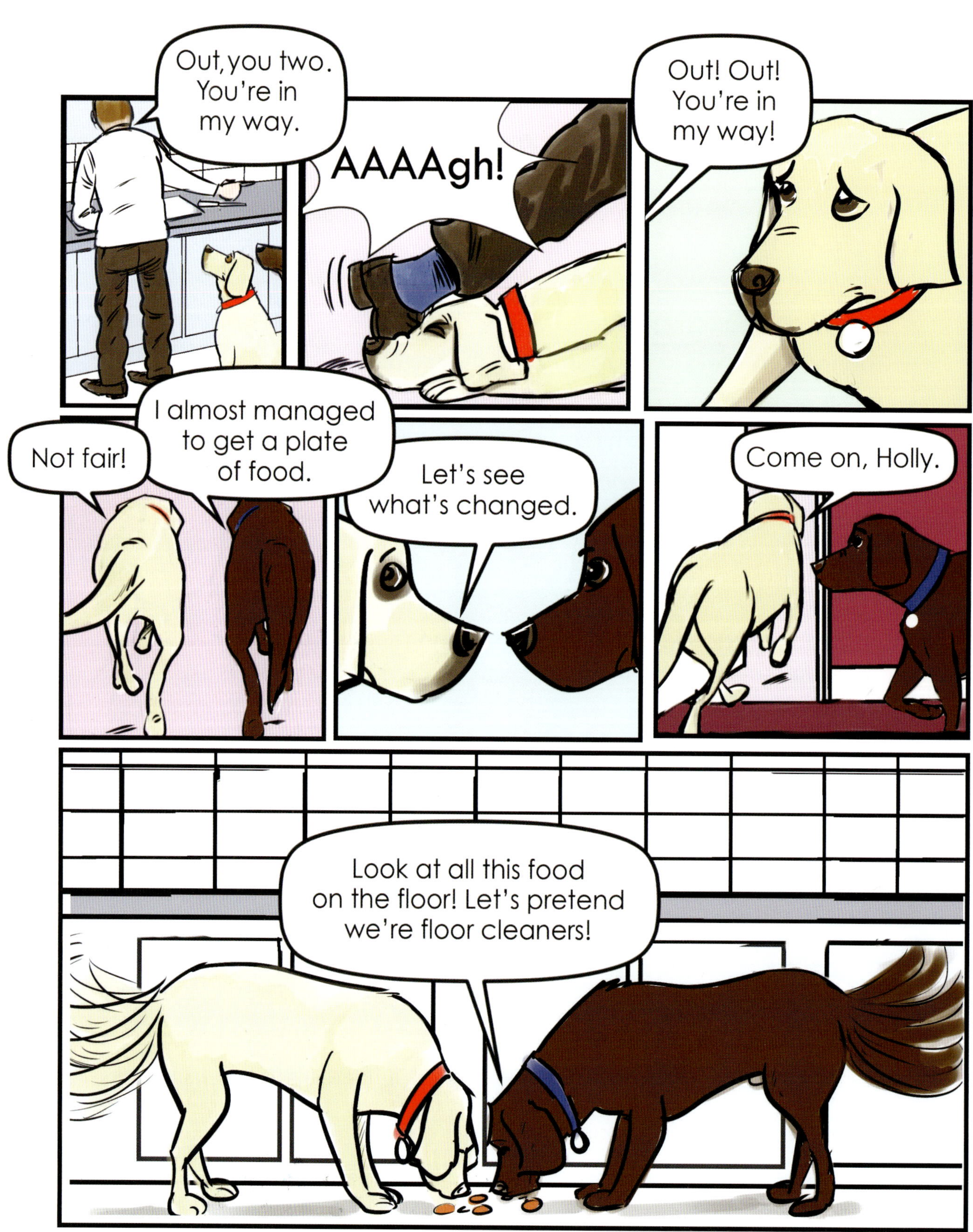

Out, you two. You're in my way.
AAAAgh!
Out! Out! You're in my way!
Not fair!
I almost managed to get a plate of food.
Let's see what's changed.
Come on, Holly.
Look at all this food on the floor! Let's pretend we're floor cleaners!

Bramble never gives up trying to help our two dogs use their memories. Holly is busy woofing at cheeky squirrels so Bramble plays a memory game with Charlie.
Look at this picture. Try to remember it. Ask yourself some questions.
Anything to do with food will get Charlie to join in.....
Ooh - biscuits in a bowl. I want to eat them. What do I ask. Sounds silly - asking yourself questions.
What is it? DUH - a bowl full of biscuits of course. I want to eat them. Breakfast was such a long time ago. I'll count them. Bramble will be pleased - I'm really good at counting now....One, two, three, four....nine biscuits in a bowl. I love biscuits - and I love 9 biscuits nine times more than just one.
What can you remember?
Nine biscuits in my bowl...
Brilliant! Clever dog. I'll magic nine biscuits for you.
Whoosh!
Yummy! I could do with a couple of biscuits.
That's not fair! I've only got one, two, three, four, five, six now. Holly didn't even do the hard remembering bit.
Never mind....I'll magic you three more so you'll still have nine biscuits. Abracadabra! These are bigger than the ones Holly took. Just as well you counted and remembered them.

31

Pairs Game

What you need:

A pack of cards with two cards of every picture.

You can download some special Magic Memory cards from www.memorysue.com.

How to play:

Spread some cards, picture side down, on a table.

Take it in turns to turn over two cards so that:
- the cards stay in the same place on the table and
- everyone can see the pictures.

When two cards match you:
- win them and
- have another go.

When the two cards don't match you:
- put them back in the same place
- your go is now finished .

The winner has the most cards at the end of the game.

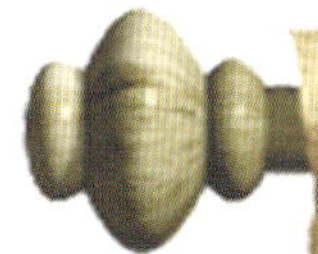

1. **When others have their turn ask yourself:**

- **What** the card is *before* they turn it over.
- **Where is** the matching card?

2. **Look for shapes and patterns** that the cards make on the table.

3. **Remind yourself** where all the cards are in between turns.

4. **Always turn over any card you're not quite sure of first.**
   If it's the wrong card, you will still have a chance of finding a different matching card.

Bramble shows how clever she is at winning this pairs game. Charlie and Holly can't concentrate like Bramble. They don't watch other people's moves so our clever Wizards's cat finds it much too easy to beat them.

I always win this.
They don't watch others having their turn.
I concentrate all the time.
I look at every single card when it's turned over.
I find patterns to remember where the cards are.
I remind myself where cards are.
A little while later our clever cat is having a winning streak.....
....But Bramble is only winning because Holly and Charlie are not thinking about the game.

Bramble likes to win...but she doesn't want it to be this easy.
Urrgh! You've made it really easy for me to win yet again. But anyone could win against you two.

Is Charlie going to do any better than Holly? Don't think so. He's turned over the same cards as Holly because he didn't watch Holly have his turn.
This is such a hard game!
Not if you concentrate and watch others having their turn. You've just turned over the same cards that Holly did.
You wasted your go. Why turn over the same cards as Holly? Cards can't magic themselves into something else!

Quiz

When I play the pairs game I will
(write the letter **T** for True or **F** for False):

.... Watch the television when it is someone else's turn.

.... Watch every single card that the others turn over.

.... Look for patterns and shapes that the cards make on the table.

.... Start talking to the person next to me when it's not my turn.

.... Turn over any card that I'm not quite sure of first- then if I'm wrong

I still have the rest of my go to find the matching card for it.

.... Think of what the card is as soon as someone touches it- I can then

test myself to see if I've remembered it right when they

turn it over!

.... Look out of the window when it's someone else's turn.

Check your answers with those at the back of the book.

All correct? Great! Colour in the next bit of Memo.

Quick Fire Numbers

For those boring queues .....

How to play:

Two people take it in turns to say a list of things as quickly as they can.

You must say:

- one of something
- then two of something else
- then three of something different and so on
- you add on your new thing at the end of the list

You are out if you are slow or forget something.

The person who remembers the most is the winner.

The winner goes on to play another person.

You make up a different list of things every time you play.

Magic Memory Tip

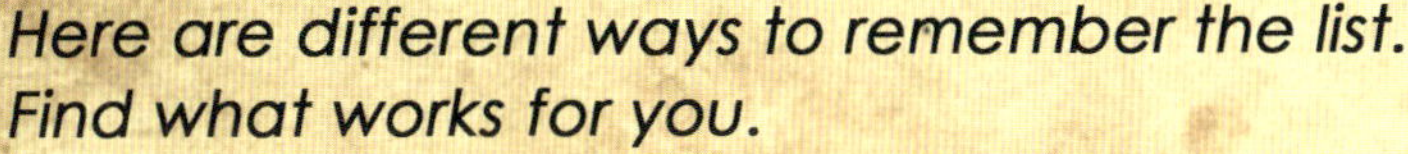

Here are different ways to remember the list. Find what works for you.

See everything in your mind:

Imagine TWO HENS when you think of 2. They could be noisily pecking the 2 or fighting over the 2. The number acts like a hook in the same way you have a coat hook at school for hanging up your coat.

See everything at different places on your way to school.

Make up your own cartoon story:

- Think of a duck.
- Then think of two hens chasing the duck.
- Then three sausages landing from the sky, flattening the hens.
- Make it colourful with a lot of action and a lot of noise!

Quick Fire Numbers

Advanced Version

You can make this much more fun by using some describing words.

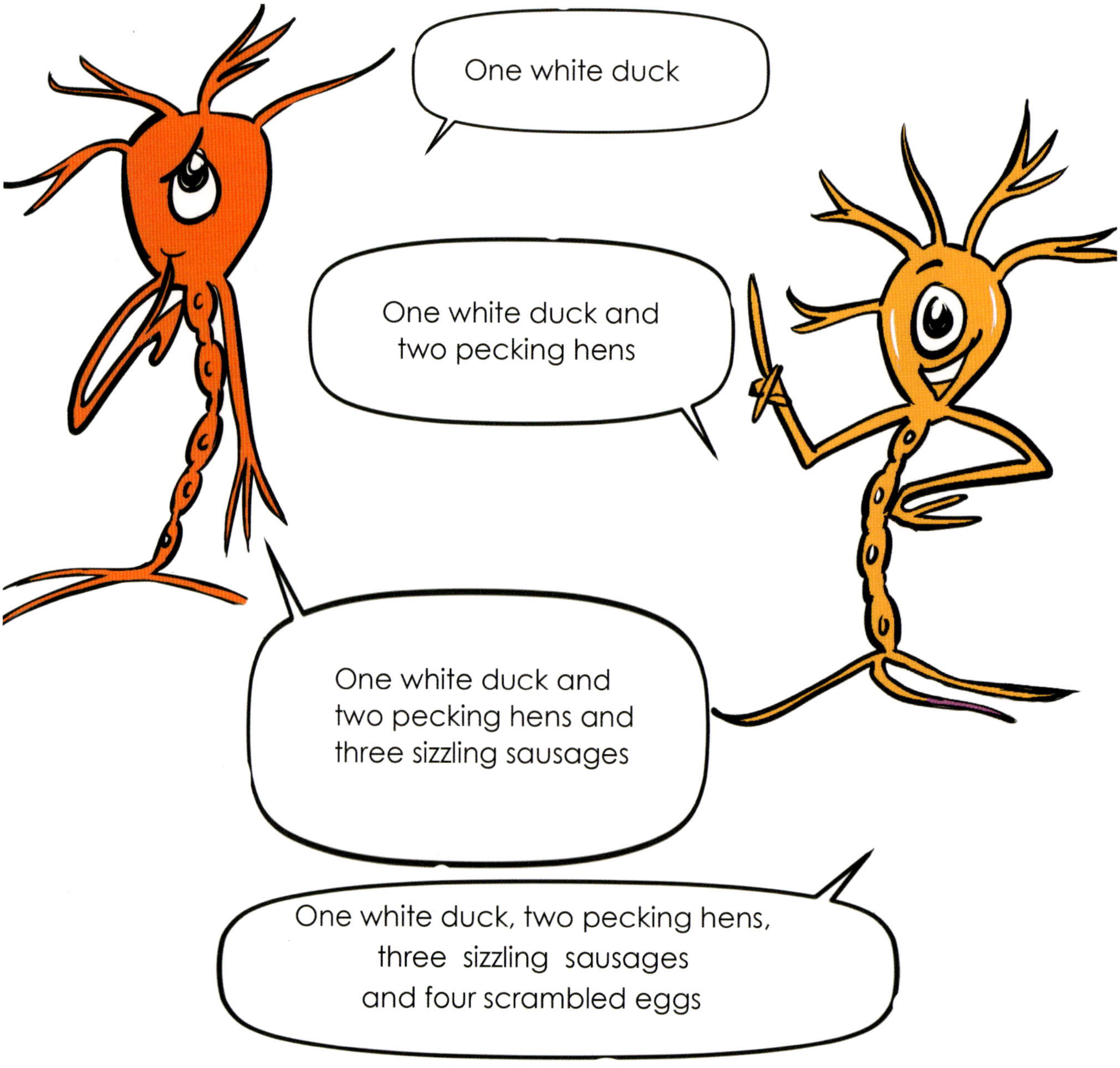

Bramble doesn't give up. She is still trying to help Charlie and Holly use their memories. She also hopes that one day they will be good enough so she'll enjoy playing with them and won't find it so easy to beat them.

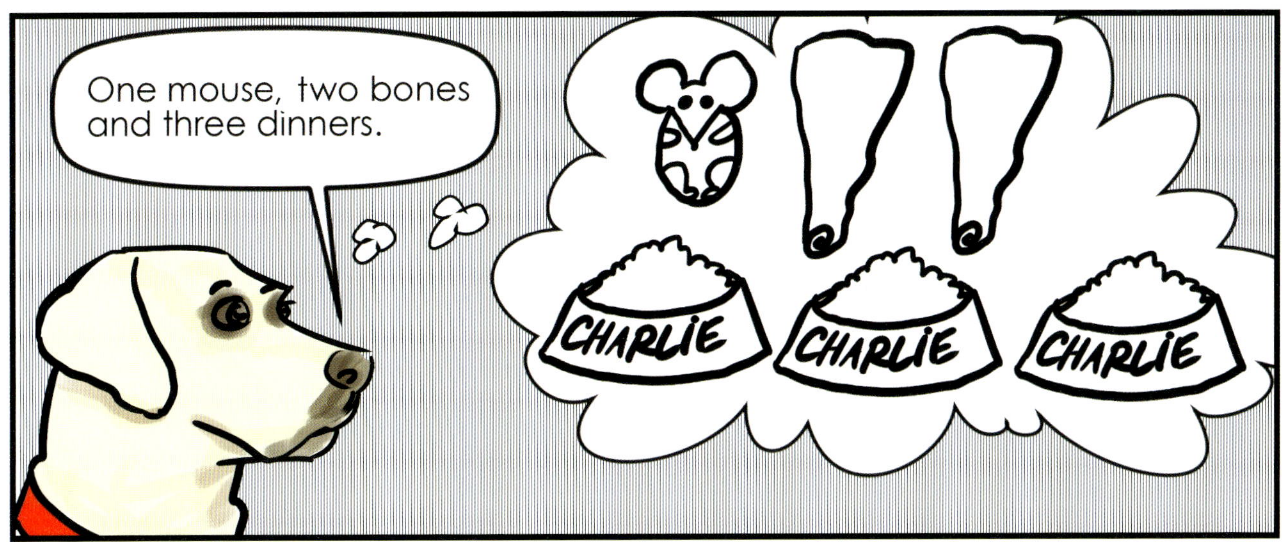

Bramble remembers things by making up a cartoon. There's lots of action, colour and noise. And it's fun.......
One mouse, two bones, three dinners and four goldfish.
....But Charlie and Holly don't use their imagination like Bramble does so they will soon make mistakes.
One mouse, two bones, three dinners, four fish......
No! That's wrong! Four **gold**fish. You're out!

Unfair! A goldfish is a fish.
One mouse, two bones, three dinners, four goldfish, and five meaty..........
Holly! Charlie! Dinner time!
Sorry Bramble, we want to eat our dinner, not think about it.
CHARLIE
CHARLIE

Quiz

When I remember a list of things I will
(write the letter **T** for True or **F** for False):

.....Make a grey picture in my mind of the first thing.

.....Think of a grey picture of the second thing next to the grey picture of the first thing.

.....Make a colour picture in my mind of the first thing.

.....Make the colour picture of the first thing do something to the colour picture of the second thing.

.....Make the colour picture of the second thing do something to the colour picture of the third thing.

.....Make up my own funny cartoon with lots of action.

.....Hear all the sounds my cartoon makes.

.....See lots of bright colours in my cartoon.

.....Imagine that I am in the cartoon and really close to everything.

.....Have fun.

.....Laugh at the funny cartoon I've made up in my mind.

Check your answers with those at the back of the book.
All correct? Great! Colour in the next bit of Memo.

Today Bramble's going to show the dogs how to chunk things. But there is one problem....the dogs' idea of chunking is different from Bramble's!
What's chunking?
I'm going to show you chunking today.
Must be huge chunks of meat. Yum, yum, yummy says my tummy!
Ooh! I love a good chunk of meat. Bramble's got it right today!
We'll start NOW. Where's our meat?
Sorry guys....but my chunking's nothing to do with meat.
What? I want a chunk of meat
That's not fair Bramble. I'm really hungry now.
Holly, let's find some chunks of meat.
No... you're playing my chunking game. I'll magic some food at the end!
Brains love patterns. You can learn things just by sorting them out and looking for patterns. It's hard to remember six things........
HOLLY

...but look! There are only two types of thing to remember. What are they?
Food!
Things for our walks!
So you know them without learning them, don't you?
I'll be a memory champion.
So what was there?
Food! .... dinner, bone....apple. Can I eat them now?
Things for walks...ball, collar and lead.
Excellent. I'll magic your own chunk of food now.
Mmmmm.. Yummy!
HOLLY
CHARLIE
HOLLY

How to play

Find a wizard
(if you can't find one any old grown-up will do).

They go into a different room to put 12 small things on a tray.
They cover the tray with a cloth.
They bring the tray into your room.
Everyone sits around the tray.

When everyone is ready and can see the tray properly
the wizard (or any old grown up) takes the cloth off the tray.

You and your friends all have one minute to remember as
many things as you can.

The wizard (or any old grown-up) then covers the tray again.

You write down all the things you remember
(wrong spellings are OK).

The winner's the one who remembers the most.

What four things are to do with food:

Food things: ____

What four things go to school in your pencil case:

Pencil case things: ____

What are the last four odd things you may find in a kitchen drawer:

Other: ____

Colour in the next bit of Memo if you got these answers:

Food: egg, red apple, cheese, orange juice.

Pencil case: pen, paper clip, rubber, pencil sharpener.

Others: ball, string, light bulb, screwdriver.

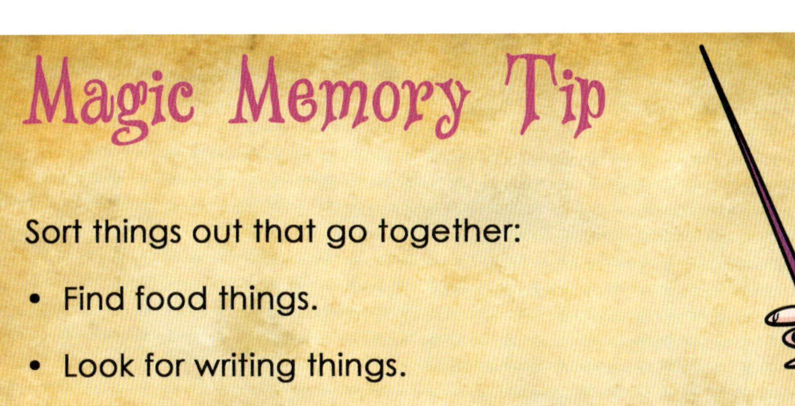

Magic Memory Tip

Sort things out that go together:

• Find food things.

• Look for writing things.

• Any odd things you can put together at the end.

This is called chunking.

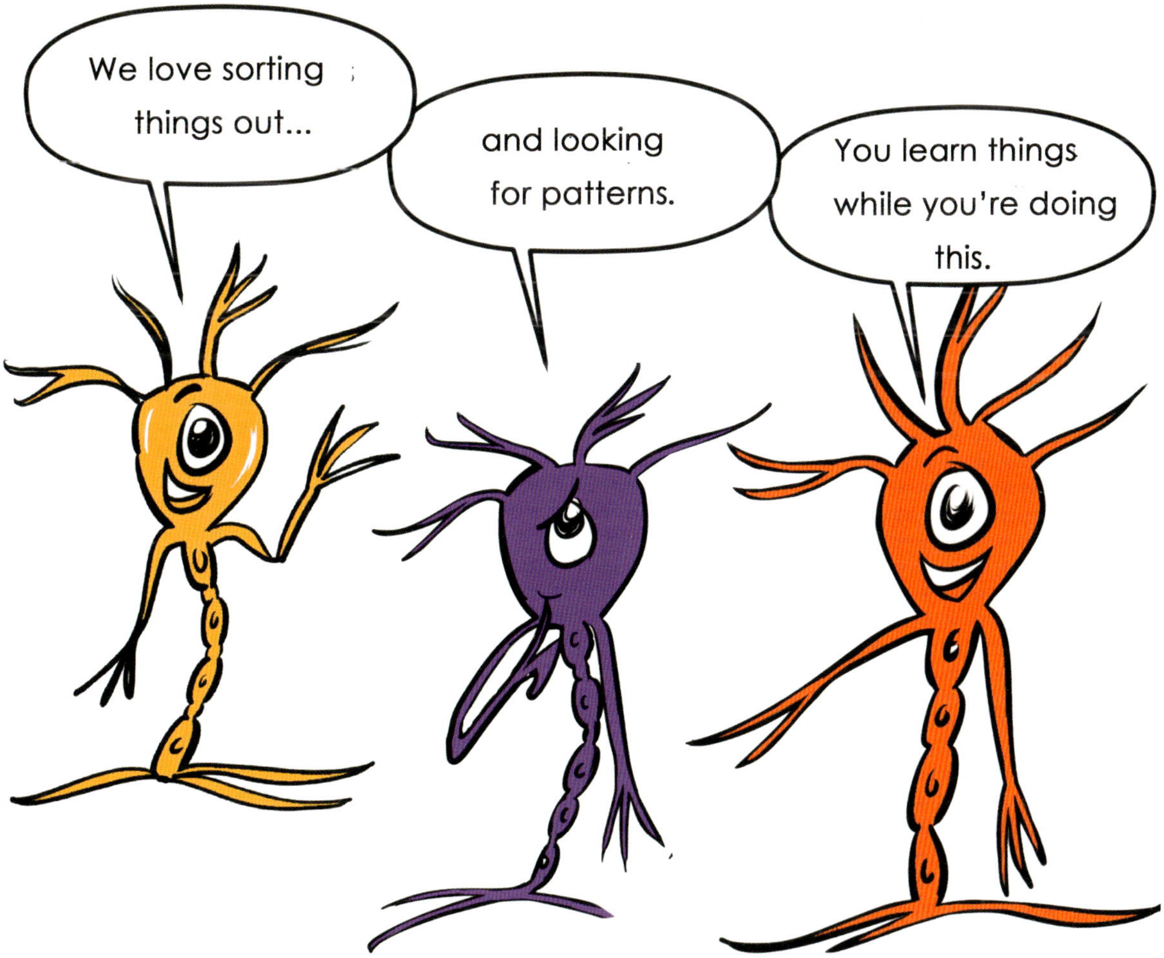

We love sorting things out...
and looking for patterns.
You learn things while you're doing this.

Kim's Game

Let's now take the food items and create a cartoon sequence with them.

Imagine the wedge of cheese falls from the air like an axe blade towards the orange juice.......

...the cheese wedge slices through the orange juice..........

.....as the orange juice falls in half the letter O falls off as an egg.......

.....the egg falls to the ground and breaks. Inside there's a red apple.

Kim's Game

Let's take the pencil case items and organise them into a cartoon sequence.

Let's imagine the fountain pen draws the paper clip..........

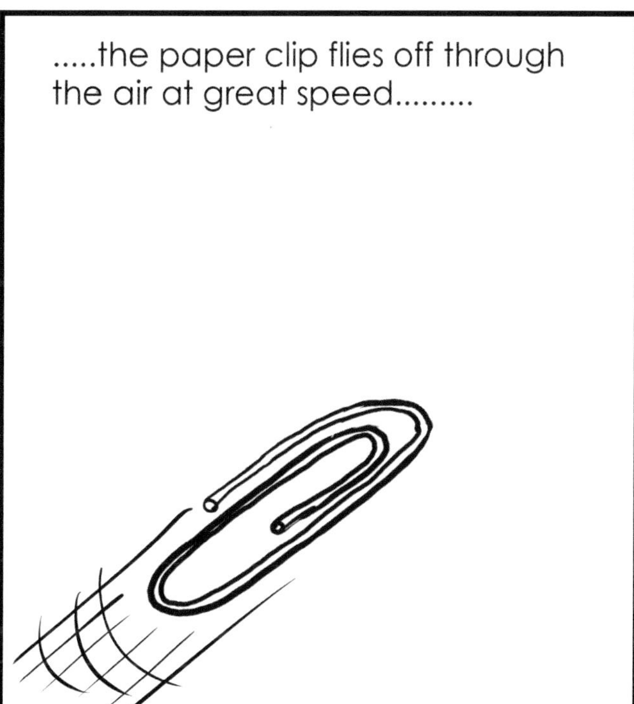

.....the paper clip flies off through the air at great speed.........

.....the paper clip hits the rubber and goes straight through it, making a hole. The rubber then magics itself into.........

......the pencil sharpener!

Kim's Game

Now let's take the drawer items and do the same.

Let's imagine the screwdriver is tied to the end of the ball of string and it's whizzing round and round. Then suddenly it breaks free and flies off at great speed.........

.....the screwdriver flies into the ball and punctures it.............

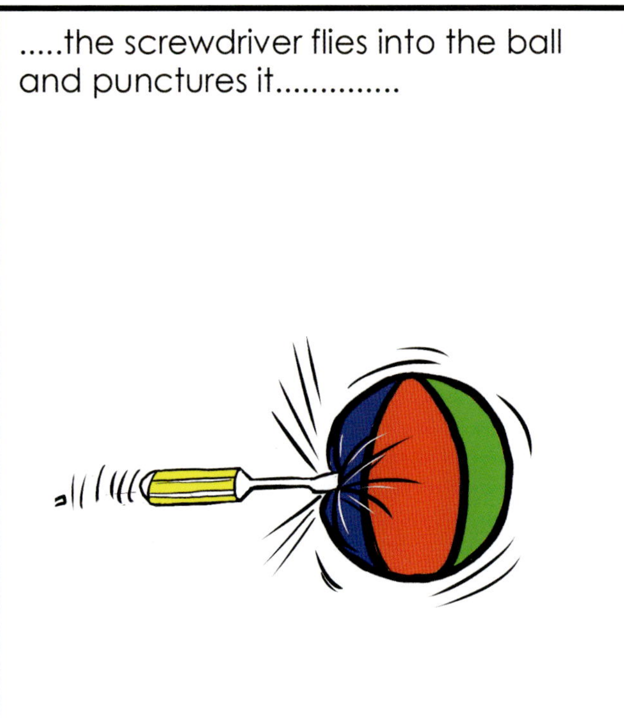

......the ball bursts and shatters and inside there is.........

........the light bulb.

Another Kim's Game to play

* The four food and drink things:

____

* The five things found in a school bag:

____

* The last three things:

____

Colour in the next bit of Memo if you got these Magic Memory Chunks.

Four food things: orange, green grapes, milk, carrot.

Five things in a school bag: scissors, book, felt tip pen, pencil, ruler.

Last three things: £1 coin, camera, safety pin.

Now cover this page. How many things can you remember?

This is how Bramble remembers the three different chunks:

She builds a tower with the food things.

She pretends she cuts a book with scissors and out jump the other writing things.

Then Bramble pretends she uses the camera to take a photograph of the safety pin stuck in a £1 coin.

Quiz

Write the letter **T** for True or **F** for False next to the things below.

Bramble showed you some very special chunks to help you remember things. What were they?

.... Chunks of chocolate bars
.... Holly's chunks of meat
.... Charlie's chunks of meat
.... Chunks of the same type of things such as a food chunk that has things like a carrot, grapes and milk.

Your brain loves:

.... To be busy.
.... Looking for patterns.
.... Looking for things that are similar.
.... Sorting things into chunks.
.... Being bored.

Your brain begins to learn things:

.... As soon as it looks for patterns.
.... When it starts sorting things into chunks.
.... When you say 'I am bored'.

Your brain finds it's quicker to learn:

.... 12 different things one after the other.
.... 3 chunks of 4 things.

**Check your answers with those at the back of the book.
All correct? Great! Colour in the next bit of Memo.**

Match the Brian Cells
to their Spooky Shadows

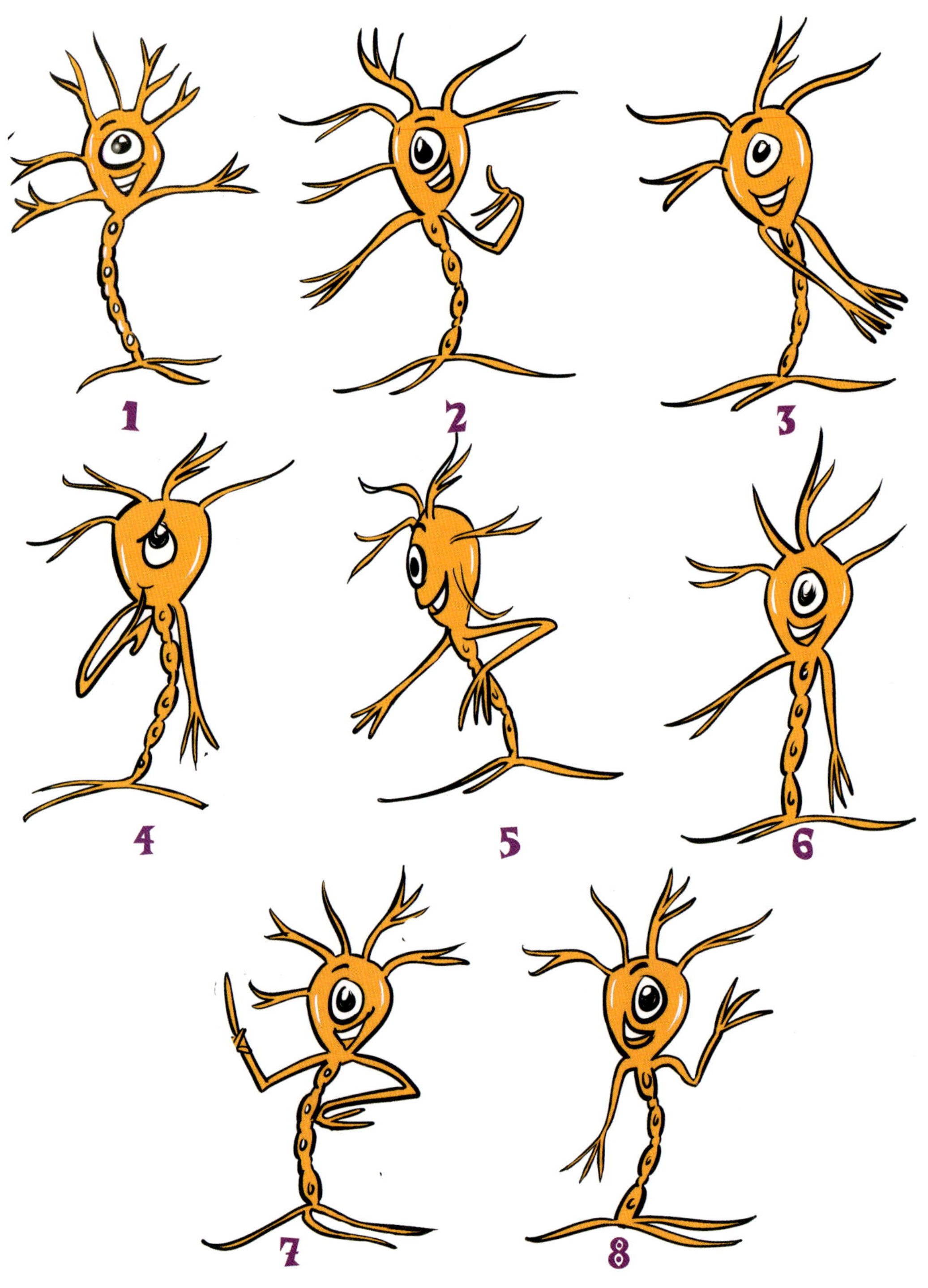

1
2
3
4
5
6
7
8

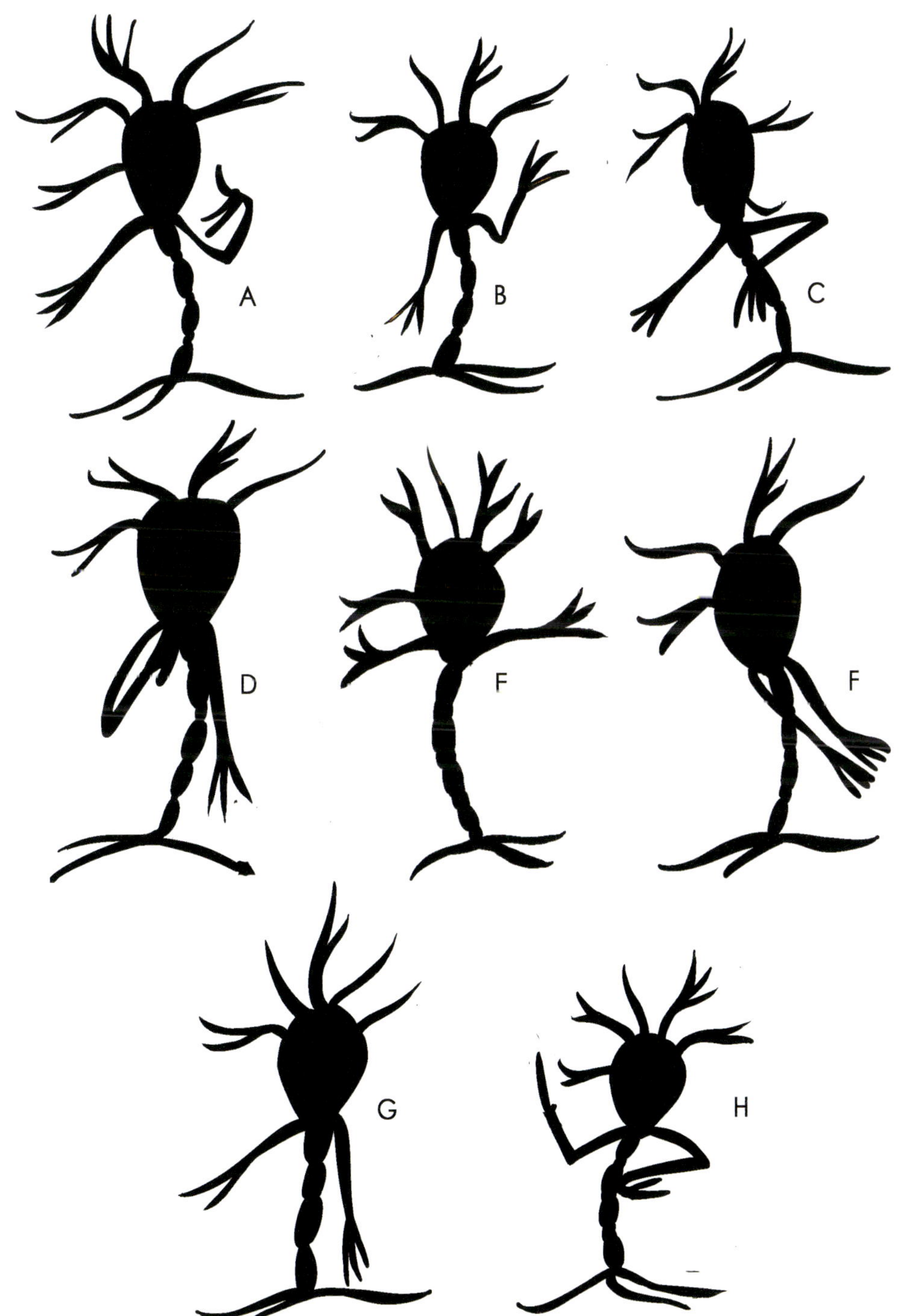

Colour in the next bit of Memo when you have matched them up.

Spellings

It's important to spell words correctly. What would happen if you spelled something wrong that you were trying to buy on the internet? You'd get the wrong thing delivered!
Holly has ordered something very special from the internet.
HOLLY
ROYAL M
What's up, Holly?
EEEK!
I ordered meaty chews and I got me two shoes...and I've got four feet anyway!
And those won't have much flavour either!

How did that happen?
Ah ha....I bet you typed **me two** instead of **meaty** and **shoes** instead of **chews**.
This mustn't happen again. You must learn how to spell.
But spellings are so hard.
My Magic Memory way is easy. Shall I show you ?
Yes please!

Wizard's Wordsearch

Find these Words in the word search: they all have the sound 'eee' in them.

be
bee
beech
beach
cathedral
Charlie
cheese
debris
easy
eat
Holly
key
peace
people
piece
pizza
police
protein
quay
queen
receive
see
sea
secret
sweet
ski
these
thief
wheeze

C	h	a	r	l	i	e	s	e	e	i	k	k	r	r
d	e	b	r	i	s	i	e	a	t	H	o	l	l	y
a	t	h	e	s	e	k	r	r	o	b	e	a	c	h
c	a	t	h	e	d	r	a	l	p	o	l	i	c	e
a	b	r	s	e	c	r	e	t	q	b	e	e	c	h
p	e	o	p	l	e	f	l	o	r	s	q	u	a	y
r	s	e	a	c	c	w	h	e	e	z	e	o	h	o
r	e	c	e	i	v	e	c	z	w	y	o	l	b	e
m	p	r	z	k	j	u	b	e	e	q	g	h	i	i
e	s	w	e	e	t	c	e	n	t	h	i	e	f	h
p	i	e	c	e	q	w	r	t	a	p	i	z	z	a
l	p	r	o	t	e	i	n	a	c	q	s	h	y	m
k	r	p	e	a	c	e	c	h	e	e	s	e	w	v
u	e	v	q	u	e	e	n	h	v	e	a	s	y	h
s	k	i	l	y	n	c	k	e	y	d	e	x	e	s

Find the five pairs of words you say in the same way but have different spellings.
The first one has been done for you:

quay/key ______________________________

____

How many different ways can you find to make the sound 'eee'?

____

Check your answers to colour in the next bit of Memo.
Look out for the Magic Memory Spelling book in 2015!

How to get going when your brain stays in bed

Ok...you're out of bed (just)! You've eaten your breakfast (sort of)! But your head feels as though it's still in bed, fast asleep. Don't worry! We all have one of those days. Use these ideas to get your
Get up and go!

FIRST AID

I'm starving.

So am I. I need fuel - like a car does.

FOOD

Send a signal to the Food Brians. Organise a proper breakfast!

GOOD FOOD = HAPPY BRIANS

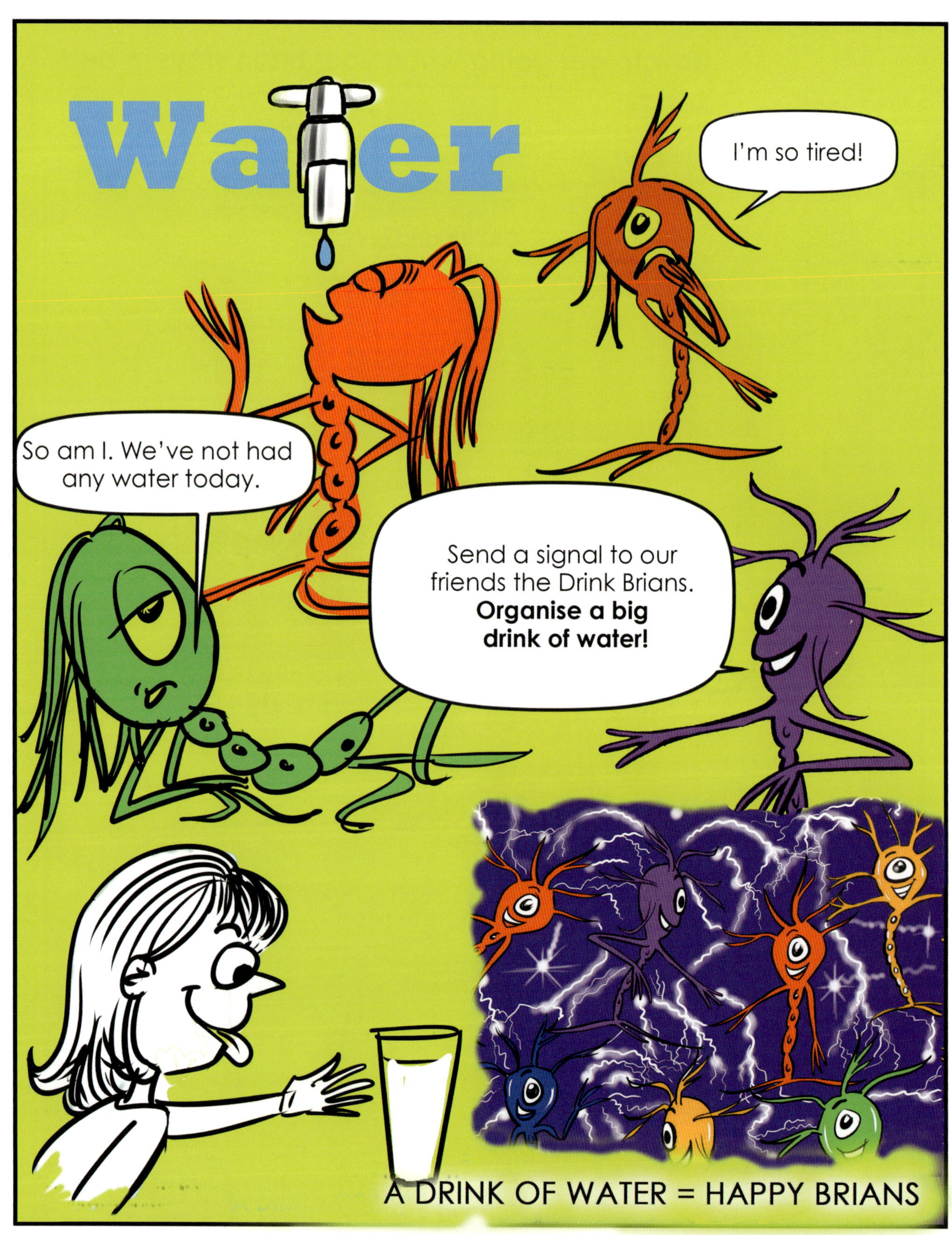
Water
I'm so tired!
So am I. We've not had any water today.
Send a signal to our friends the Drink Brians.
Organise a big drink of water!
A DRINK OF WATER = HAPPY BRIANS

The Brain food you can't see.

FRESH AIR

O_2xygen

Magic Brain Fact

It's not just food and water that feeds your brain.
It needs food that you can't see such as fresh air.
The oxygen in fresh air gives your brain energy.

When you sit down for a long time your heart beats slowly. So there's less blood and less oxygen getting to your brain.

TAKE A BREAK:

Do one of these:
- Stand up and sit down six times
- Skip around the room.
- Do six star jumps
- Play some music and dance!

Sleep
I'm so sleepy.
So am I.
Tell me about it! We couldn't get our cleaning jobs done. Now his memories are all over the place.
It's his fault - watching that late night movie.
LATE NIGHT FILM
Go to bed earlier tonight to give your Brian Cells enough time to finish all their cleaning jobs. You and your Brian Cells will then be full of energy for tomorrow.
That was a great night's sleep. Now I feel full of energy!

Quiz

What are the best ways to get your Brian Cells sparking and learning things?
(Write the letter **T** for True or **F** for False):

.... Eat breakfast

.... Drink water

.... Watch television

.... Go to bed early

.... Get some fresh air

.... Say 'I'm fed up'

Did you find all four true things?

Check your answers with those

at the back of the book.

All correct? Great!   Colour in the next bit of Memo.

Meanwhile at the Wizard's Castle......
Memo's almost better! Children's Magic Memories are making her well again.
So can I go home now?
They're doing a great job.
Sweet
Er..Well not quite yet. Just look at this.... They still don't know their multiplication tables.....
Charlie and Holly are independent dogs and like to do their own shopping. Today Charlie is going to order lots of bones. He is fed up of running out of them.
One bone every day for 6 weeks. Now how many is that?
A lot of bones. Yummy!
But how many do I order?
Duh......
I know. Let's put 'Lots of' on the order form!
That's a brilliant idea, Holly.
Sigh!

Wizard's Sudoku

This is a sudoku with a difference: all the numbers are in the 2 x table: 1 x 2 =2   2 x 2 =4   3 x 2 =6   4 x 2 =8   5 x 2 =10   6 x 2 =12

Fill in the grid so that every row, every column and every box has the numbers 2, 4, 6, 8, 10, 12.

12	8		2		6
	10				
		8	12		
6		10	8		
	6		10	4	
10				8	2

Check your answers with those at the back of the book
Are they right? Great! Colour in the next bit of Memo.

Wizard's Puzzle

There are three numbers missing in the wheel. What are they?

Hint – they are all in the three times table!

When you get them right (answers are at the back) colour in the next bit of Memo

To play more games like these, look out for the **Magic Memory Tables Fun** book in 2015.

Even the dogs need a good night's sleep after a busy day. It gives them energy to have even more fun the next day.
Charlie and Holly are running around chasing a ball in the park.

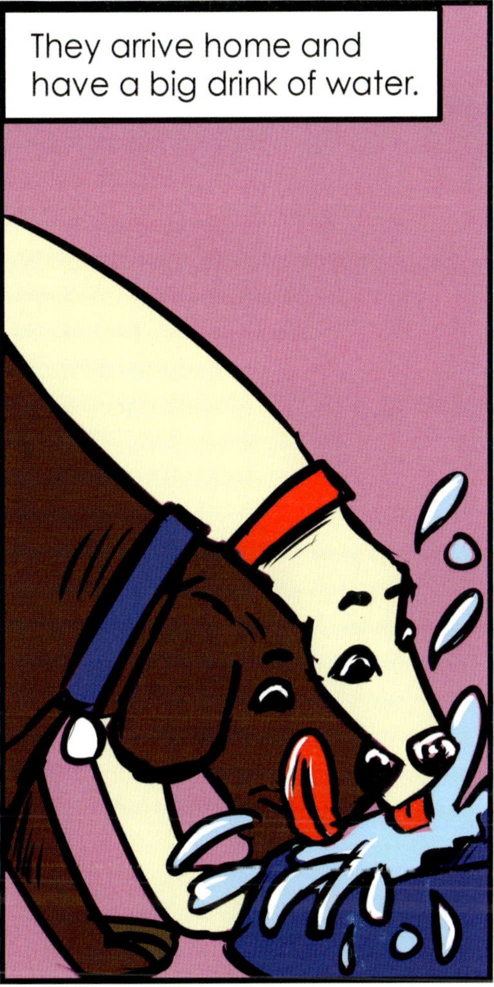

They arrive home and have a big drink of water.

HOLLY
CHARLIE
I do like to have a good sleep after a busy day.
I want lots of energy for my busy day tomorrow!

How Memory Champions remember PIN Numbers

Draw pictures, using the shape of the number,
for every number below. A swan looks like a number 2.
This has been done for you.

1 =

7 =

2 =

8 =

3 =

9 =

4 =

0 =

5 =

There are no right or wrong answers
for this. Everyone thinks of different
pictures when they see a number.
Find out what pictures work best for
YOU. On the next two pages are
pictures that memory champions use.

6 =

Circle the pictures that sort of look like 1.
How many are there?____

Circle the pictures that sort of look like 2.
How many are there?____

Circle the pictures that sort of look like 3.
How many are there?____

Circle the pictures that sort of look like 4.
How many are there?____

Circle the pictures that sort of look like 5.
How many are there?____

Circle the pictures that sort of look like 8.
How many are there?____

Circle the pictures that sort of look like 6.
How many are there?____

Circle the pictures that sort of look like 9.
How many are there?____

Circle the pictures that sort of look like 7.
How many are there?____

Circle the pictures that sort of look like 0.
How many are there?____

To colour in the next bit of Memo check your answers.

THIS SECRET CODE BELONGS TO

....

Draw your pictures for your number shape code. Or, if you want to, write down what you will use.

1 =

2 =

3 =

4 =

5 =

6 =

7 =

8 =

9 =

0 =

1 = ______________   6 = ______________

2= ______________   7 = ______________

3 = ______________   8 = ______________

4 = ______________   9 = ______________

5 = ______________   0 = ______________

Playing with the Number Shape Code

Memory champions make up cartoon stories to remember number pictures in the right order.

What you do is:

- Turn the number into its picture (using your code).
- Make your first number picture do something to your second number picture. You want bright colours, lots of action and noise.
- Now make your second number picture do something with your third number picture and so on.

The number code used here is:

1 = candle	6 = elephant (trunk)
2 = swan	7 = boomerang
3 = heart	8 = snowman
4 = yacht	9 = (smoking) pipe
5 = skier	0 = football

To remember the number **17981**

The pictures used here are:

1 = candle   7= boomerang   8 = snowman   9 = pipe

If yours is different, use it. You'll remember it better.

This gives you the number:

1 7 9 8 1

Bramble plays the number shape code game with the clever dogs.

It's now time to save the last bit of Memo, my clever little Mnemons! You have almost done it!

All you have to do now is to make up three different cartoon stories for these three different pin numbers.

Remember:

• Use your own code to turn every number into its picture.

• Then join up the 4 numbers in each pin number by making up your own cartoon story.

8905

6702

6134

There are some ideas at the back of the book
but your own special number code will work
better for you.

When you've made up cartoons, colour in the
last bit of Memo.

You've done it!

You've saved her!

Acknowledgements

This book is the culmination of over twenty years work in the field of memory. During that time I have extensively researched and experimented with numerous memory systems and finding the right environment for learning. There have been so many people who have been influential along my journey that it is impossible to mention them all. But here are the ones that immediately spring to mind:

My parents: for playing all those memory games with me and for giving me the necessary environment that encouraged an enquiring mind.

Tony Buzan, founder of the World Memory Championships, whose books 'Use your Memory' and 'Master your Memory' set me on this exciting journey and for the brainstorming sessions we had in developing the most advanced memory system in the world today: the SEM3 system.

Chris Day of Filament Publishing: for his wonderful support, ideas and all our brain storming sessions that enabled my original manuscript to evolve into this book.

Rick Coleman: for his invaluable and highly imaginative illustrations that brought the whole book to life.
Fleur Iggulden and Jane Mallin for their editing and ideas that influenced the final book.

Sandra Taylor, headmistress (now retired) of Newberries Primary School, Radlett: for her enthusiasm with the Junior Memory Challenge, her invaluable feedback and her subsequent ideas and encouragement.
My sister, Pamela Hunt, and my friends who proof read and shared their ideas: Julian Fenton, Marsha Gordon, Sue Gordon, Liz Hartnett, Jill Holden, Sue Justice, Gill Westbrook.

My daughters: Carolyn, Helen and Fiona for all their support, patience, imaginative ideas, contributions as well as proof reading – and of course for being guinea pigs for my ideas over the years.

My wonderful husband, John, who has given me the most amazing support throughout this whole journey, without whom this book would never have been finished.

Afterword for parents and teachers

Learning how to use one's memory is probably the most important life skill that any human being undertakes. Whatever we do draws to a greater or lesser extent on our memory of how – or indeed whether – to do something. Even finding something out for the first time will draw on basic learnt skills.

Humans, like other animals, were designed to develop their memories through play, usually with some assistance from their parents. Yet in this modern electronic age many children do not have the privilege of learning how to use their memories through play.

Somehow they are expected to know instinctively how to use their memories. Or perhaps they are meant to assume that they don't need to develop a memory as they, just like their computers, have one inbuilt. Problems can then occur at school when, without having developed the necessary tools, they are expected to know how to learn things.

We all know of children who are falling between the cracks of the educational system. This is usually through no fault of their own – or that of the teachers. Typically, these are children who are unable to keep up with their peers through being unable to learn things quickly enough. As they fall behind, they become disenchanted with the educational system and then the real problems begin. Remedial action rarely stresses the need to improve memory – or appreciates that the problem could have been avoided in the first place if the child had developed their memory as so many of their ancestors did.

This series of books has been written to show children of all ages how to use their memories far more effectively. As they read the books and play the games, children will learn how to use their memories in a comfortable, safe and fun environment. They will learn through playing and having fun – which is, after all, how most of the animal kingdom learns. They'll be seeing how two loveable but rather stupid dogs are learning how to use their memories. They will meet up with Brian Cells, who bear an uncanny resemblance to brain cells and live in their brains. All this is in an easy going cartoon style book that will appeal to all readers. Their newly learned skills will be transferable to all areas of their lives, not just to their school work.

The books don't just cover memory techniques in isolation. The emphasis is on getting the right environment for learning. It is now well established that the best way to learn anything is by being in the right state of mind: by being in a positive emotional state. Science has now substantiated what educators have always known. Recent research has discovered that the heart has its own brain with its own intricate network of neurons, neurotransmitters, proteins and support cells. The 40,000 sensory neurons hold memories: short-term and long-term.
This heart-brain is a sophisticated information encoding and processing centre in its own right. There are more messages that go from the heart to the brain than from the brain to the heart. These signals from the heart to the brain have a significant effect on how the brain works: not just memory but perception, problem-solving and concentration . So the most effective learning will undoubtedly take place when there is a positive emotional state (cortical facilitation).

The flip side is that stress hormones, released in the well-known fight/flight syndrome, are now known to switch off the higher levels of the brain, to enable the basic survival instinct to take over (cortical inhibition). So a stressed brain is, in most cases, incapable of storing new information. Nowadays, stress isn't usually triggered by life threatening things, such as the sabre toothed tiger starting to attack, but by relatively trivial things. But however that stress is triggered, it still has the same physiological effect on the body. Hence the importance of children being raised and educated in a safe, stress free environment and to be given the support that they need.

And why is it important to have a good memory? Well, recent research has indicated that the most accurate predictor of a child's future academic success is how good their working (short term) memory is. And you could also ask Charlie and Holly whether they are happier now they can remember where they buried their bones…

Sue Whiting
Hertfordshire 16th December 2014
www.memorysue.com

References
i   Neurocardiology: Anatomical and Functional Principles By J. Andrew Armour, M.D., Ph.D.
ii Heart–Brain Neurodynamics: Making of Emotions By Rollin McCraty, Ph.D.
iii Working Memory & Learning:A Practical Guide for Teachers
    By Susan E Gathercole & Tracy Packiam Alloway.

About the author

Dr Sue Whiting

Dr Sue Whiting, Memory Grand Master and five times (1994 -1998) Women's World Memory Champion, has more than 20 years' extensive experience in the field of memory at all levels having lectured and coached a wide range of clients in practical memory techniques and strategies to solve their memory and learning problems. A qualified Chartered Accountant and Chartered Tax Adviser (though no longer practising), Sue now works as a writer, speaker, coach and independent memory consultant.

Sue became interested in how the memory works soon after her children arrived. A career break enabled her to develop her interest, become a Memory Grand Master and the Women's World Memory champion. In doing so, Sue realised that all the hard study that she had done to pass her university and professional exams could have been much more effective.

Sue spearheaded the first ever UK schools' memory championships when she devised and wrote all the material and training packs for the 2007/2008 Junior Memory Challenge. Her work extended to conducting pre-competition Irials as well as being arbiter for the final, held at Imperial College, London in March 2008. Year 4 children from sixty primary schools participated and the positive feedback received showed the tremendous demand there was for teaching children how to use their memories effectively.

Sue has spoken in primary schools (even teaching some of the teachers!) and also conducted the popular Wizard of Spells lectures held at the Science Museum in August 2012. Her ideas for the children's Wizard of Spells series of books were developed from these experiences.

With Sue's scientific background (the Dr refers to D. Phil in Astrophysics from Oxford University) she naturally keeps up to date with recent developments being made in neuroscience.

www.memorysue.com

About the illustrator

Rick Coleman

Rick has been working as a full time caricaturist and cartoonist for 20 years in the studio and on-the-spot at corporate events. His studio work involves private and commercial commissions of caricatures from photos and commissions for magazines and newspapers. A major client is the Armed Forces and he has established himself as one of the leading artists producing Officers' Mess Caricature Paintings. There are now over 150 paintings of up to sixty people hanging in messes around the world. Rick was the gag cartoonist for Sport First newspaper for two years with 'Rick's Sporting View'. He has been the cartoonist for Quest magazine since 1999. He had caricatures commissioned by 'This Morning' show for the last series of ' I'm a Celebrity Get Me Out of Here' and has been producing comic strip art for a Talk Sport radio advertising campaign. His work regularly appears in ITN and Channel 4 News items.

He recently appeared as a guest on the Alan Titchmarsh show.

When working on-the-spot, either traditionally or digitally, Rick's style is funny and complimentary, making him a big favourite at weddings and other celebrations. He likes to create a whole picture portraying a full body caricature usually involving a hobby, pastime or themed to your event. His live work takes him to all types of events across the country and abroad, including exhibitions, grand prix, conferences, weddings, bar and bat mitzvahs, product launches, golf days. When booking a caricaturist to work at your event please bear in mind that he can draw ten to fifteen people in an hour. If you have a specific number of people that must be drawn please consult Rick on the feasibility first.

Rick has a list of top quality caricaturists he can call upon to help with the work load. Whether it's a massive event or a small gathering your guests will be entertained with funny fantastic caricatures creating a unique memento to remember the event by.

www.caricature.co.uk/

Review by David Taylor, MA (Oxon), PGCE, formerly Director of Inspection at Ofsted.

This book takes as its credo that the training of children's memories is a valuable enterprise: good in itself but also having potential spin-offs across the field of educational activity. I would find it impossible to disagree with this belief, and also impossible to argue against a view that the importance of the memory has been significantly – woefully, even – neglected in our formal educational system, with the effect that many of our young people grow up with scant resources for learning, memorising or revising crucial information. Hence the aims of this book are admirable and its author (and illustrator) are to be commended for addressing the problem, but still more so for doing so in a way which shows a particularly good grasp of how to engage the hearts as well as the minds of a young readership.

Visually, the book is arresting and appealing from the outset, with the 'magical environment' and the use of cats and dogs (sure-fire winners for most children)…. Cartoon sequences and speech bubbles are used effectively, and the brain cells (called throughout …'Brian Cells') have a distinctive and suitably memorable appearance. But the real heartbeat of the book is the series of brain activities, which have been devised with much skill to introduce a range of proven memory techniques – and in these the visual flair is not just pleasing to the eye but has a real point in relation to the stimulating of children's imagination in aid of their developing the intended skills. This works particularly well for the creation of stories to develop recall of objects and sequences – techniques which have been demonstrated and expounded with such great success by Tony Buzan and Dominic O'Brien, for example.

Together with narrative interest created by the adventures of Bramble the cat and the labradors Charlie and Holly, the idea that the life and health of Memo, the Memory Monster, depend on the children's efforts to complete the activities successfully, is a neat one, and the gradual colouring in of Memo's picture helps to sustain momentum…. The activities generally are well pitched for inquisitive pre-teens, and they do test a range of different skills, including multiplication and spelling – although it is helpful to know that this book will be supplemented by others specialising in the discrete areas. …

Overall, there is a great deal to enjoy and admire, and the value is heavily underscored by the author's evident personal credentials, both as memory champion and educationalist with a firm grasp of classroom realities. Her ideas have been splendidly complemented by her excellent artistic collaborator. I can think of many upper primary teachers who will wish to use this with their classes, and many others who should do so – and it will also be a boon to parents who wish to support their children's learning at home.

Answers

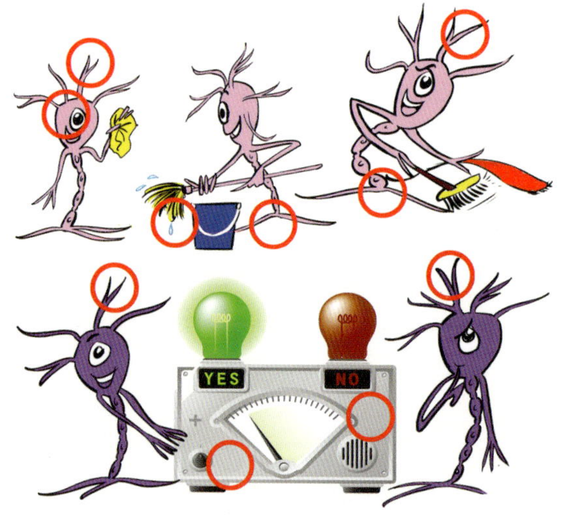

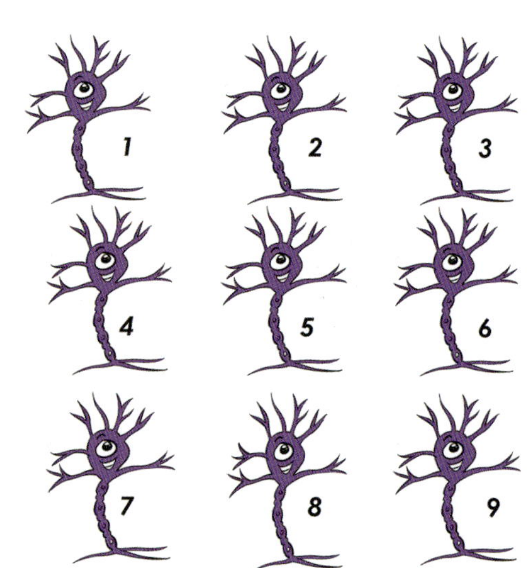

Page 17   Quiz T F T T F T F T T

Page 35   Quiz F T T F T T F

Page 42   Quiz F F T T T T T T T T

Page 53   QUIZ Chunks:F F F T

Your brain loves: T T T T F

Your brain begins to learn…: T T F

Your brain finds it's quicker to learn: F T

Page 55   Match the Brian Cells to their Spooky Shadows

1 E, 2 A, 3 F, 4 D, 5 C, 6 G, 7 H, 8 B

Page 58

The five pairs of words are:

quay/key   be/bee   beech/beach   peace/piece   sea/see

There are 15 different ways to spell 'eee' sound here.

Though it's OK if you want to count wheeze and cheese as the same spelling (ee-e) and you may want to count easy as being a different way! Holly is said with the 'eee' sound if you were calling her in the park.

As long as you got more than ten you can colour in the last bit of Memo.

ea eat sea peace beach easy

ie Charlie thief piece

y Holly

ei protein receive

ey key

ay quay

ice police

eese cheese

eeze wheeze

ese these

i   ski pizza

e be cathedral

ee queen sweet

is   debris

eo   people

C	h	a	r	l	i	e	s	e	e	i	k	k	r	r
d	e	b	r	i	s	i	e	a	t	H	o	l	l	y
a	t	h	e	s	e	k	r	r	o	b	e	a	c	h
c	a	t	h	e	d	r	a	l	p	o	l	i	c	e
a	b	r	s	e	c	r	e	t	q	b	e	e	c	h
p	e	o	p	l	e	f	l	o	r	s	q	u	a	y
r	s	e	a	c	c	w	h	e	e	z	e	o	h	o
r	e	c	e	i	v	e	c	z	w	y	o	l	b	e
m	p	r	z	k	j	u	b	e	e	q	g	h	i	i
e	s	w	e	e	t	c	e	n	t	h	i	e	f	h
p	i	e	c	e	q	w	r	t	a	p	i	z	z	a
l	p	r	o	t	e	i	n	a	c	q	s	h	y	m
k	r	p	e	a	c	e	c	h	e	e	s	e	w	v
u	e	v	q	u	e	e	n	h	v	e	a	s	y	h
s	k	i	l	y	n	c	k	e	y	d	e	x	e	s

Page 63 The best ways to get your Brian Cells sparking …

T T F T T F

Page 65 Wizard's Sudoku

12	8	4	2	10	6
2	10	6	4	12	8
4	2	8	12	6	10
6	12	10	8	2	4
8	6	2	10	4	12
10	4	12	6	8	2

Page 66 Wizard's Puzzle

Page 70/71

0 - there are two: a rubber ring, a doughnut

1- there are two: pen, candle

2- there are two: two swans

3- there are four : heart, seahorse, a banana skin and a furry animal with a long tail

4- there are two: a yacht and a cactus

5- there is one: a man with a funny hairstyle and a big nose

6- there are two: a padlock and a ballet dancer with her arm above her head

7- there are four: a boomerang, two different street lamps, a man with a long scarf

8- there are two: a snowman and a racetrack

9- there are three: a pipe, a golf club, a hose pipe

8905 Suggested answer:

Snowman (8) has a pipe (9).

Out of the pipe shoots a football (0).

The football is caught by superman (5) as he flies past.

6702 Suggested answer:

An elephant (6) throws a boomerang (7).

The boomerang hits a football (0).

Out of the football flies a swan (2).

6134 Suggested answer:

An elephant's trunk (6) picks up a pen (1).

The pen draws a heart (3).

The heart (3) then magics itself into a yacht (4).

Published by Filament Publishing Ltd

16, Croydon Road, Waddon, Croydon, Surrey CR04PA

+44 (0)208 688 2598   www.filamentpublishing.com